KIDZBIZ

FUN
to
MAKE

Gillian Souter

Off the Shelf Publishing

BEFORE YOU START...

Before you throw out those cereal boxes or egg cartons, just think what you could make with them. Here are ideas for lots of amazing projects that you can construct using simple bits and pieces. There are pictures to give you some ideas, but it's fun to make up your own designs and colour schemes.

Some of these projects can get a bit messy, so keep your work area clean and cover it with scrap paper before any painting. Use non-toxic paints such as acrylics or poster paints.

If you need to draw a circle, draw around a glass or another round object, or use a pair of compasses.

Ask for an adult's help if you need to use a craft knife or the kitchen oven.

First published in 2001 by
Off the Shelf Publishing
32 Thomas Street
Lewisham NSW 2049
Australia

Projects, text and layout
copyright © 2001 Off the Shelf Publishing
Line illustrations by Clare Watson
Photographs by Andre Martin

Contents

Odds and Ends

Lots of things that we throw out can be made into great craft projects. Keep a junk box and start collecting.

It's useful to have different types of paper, thin card and cardboard. Save cereal boxes and greetings cards. You could paint scrap paper instead of buying coloured paper.

Keep cardboard rolls of all sizes, from toilet rolls, kitchen towels and mailing tubes. Empty matchboxes, plastic bottles, egg cartons and corks are all useful.

When you lose a sock, don't throw out the other one - make a sock puppet!

There are some things that you might need to buy: drinking straws, pipe cleaners (or chenilles), modelling clay, paper cups and plates are all used in this book.

Portrait Pics

Frame mini portraits of your friends or pets with coloured ice cream sticks.

1 Measure and mark a 10 cm square on a piece of white cardboard. Cut it out.

2 Draw a picture in the centre of the square and colour it with paints or felt pens.

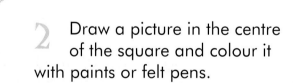

3 Cut a piece of string or thread and glue it at the top of the square to make a hanging loop.

4 You can buy ice cream sticks in packets at a craft shop. Paint eight sticks and let them dry.

5 Glue two sticks along the top and two along the bottom of the square. Glue on two more at each side.

You might like to draw on paper and stick this onto cardboard.

Pen Minder

This spiky creature could be a hedgehog, a porcupine or even an echidna. Whatever it is, it's very useful!

YOU WILL NEED

a plastic bag
air-drying clay
a knife
pencils or pens
acrylic paint
varnish
a paintbrush

1 Put a large plastic bag over your work area. Roll a large ball of clay for the body and a smaller one for the head. Shape the head with your fingers.

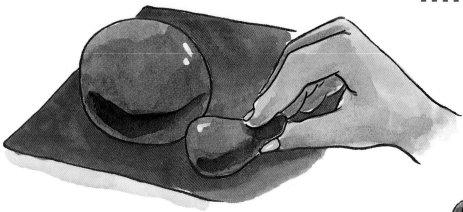

2 Roll four small balls of clay and shape each one into a paw. Use the blunt edge of a knife to mark the toes.

3 Press the head and paws frimly onto the body. Use the end of a pen lid to mark eyes on the head.

8

4 Push a pencil into the body and twist it gently. Make more holes like this, taking care that they aren't too close together.

5 Leave the model in a warm, dry place until it is completely hard. Paint it a bright colour and then brush on a coat of varnish.

If a piece breaks off when the clay is drying, just glue it back on!

9

Take Your Place

Make your own
placemat to use at the
dinner table.

1   Cut out two 37 x 27 cm rectangles
of fabric. Lay a small plate upside
down on one piece and draw around it
with chalk.

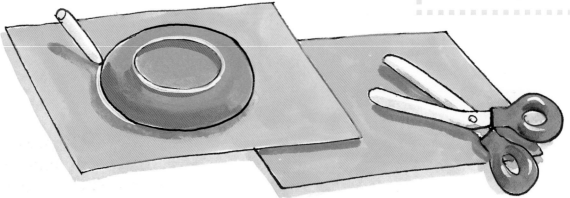

2   Draw a knife and fork
with the chalk. Thread
a needle and knot one end.

3   Sew along the chalk lines
with small, even stitches.
Hide any knots at the back.

4   Lay the two pieces of fabric together with the stitching on top. Pin a length of bias binding around the edges.

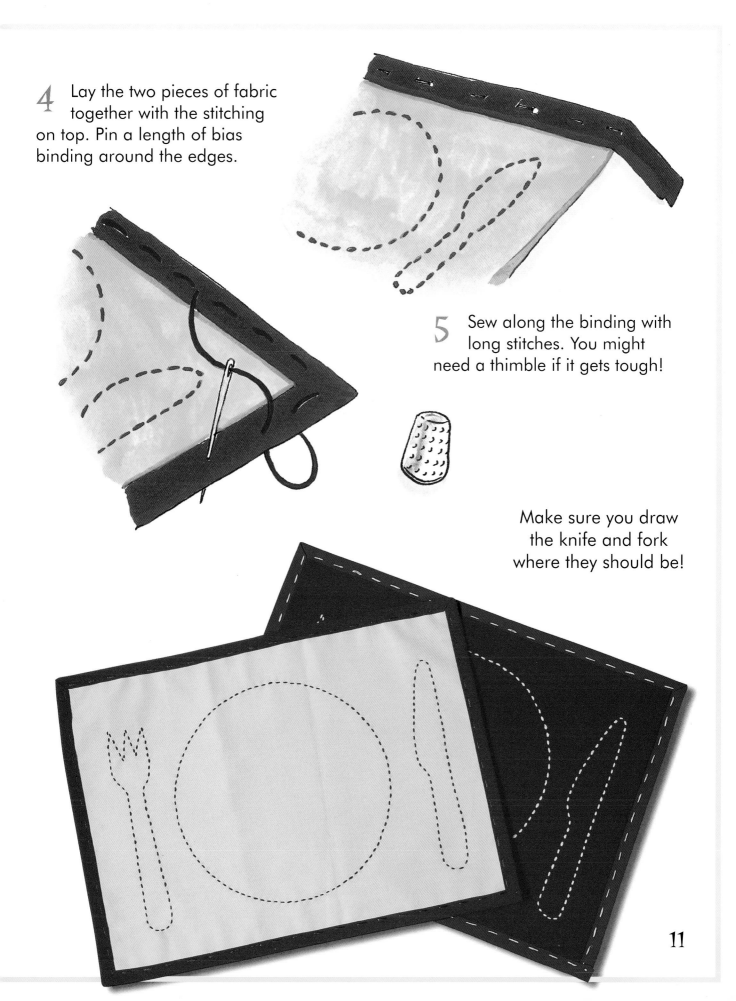

5   Sew along the binding with long stitches. You might need a thimble if it gets tough!

Make sure you draw the knife and fork where they should be!

Pet Shakes

Make lots of noise with these papier-mâché critters.

1 Roll two balls of plasticine, one larger than the other. Stick them together to make an animal shape.

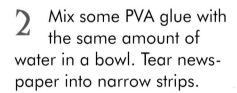

2 Mix some PVA glue with the same amount of water in a bowl. Tear newspaper into narrow strips.

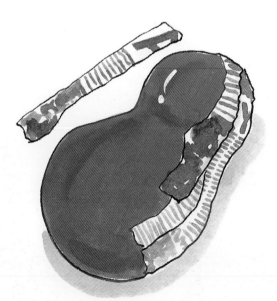

3 Dip each strip in the paste and stick it around the plasticine shape, overlapping the strips as you work. Cover the shape with five layers of strips and leave it to dry completely.

4 Ask a grown-up to cut the shape in half lengthwise with a sharp knife. Carefully pull out the plasticine.

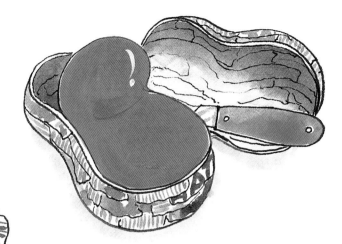

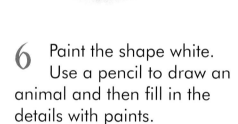

5 Put a spoonful of dry rice in one half and tape the halves together with masking tape. Paste newspaper strips over the join and let it dry.

6 Paint the shape white. Use a pencil to draw an animal and then fill in the details with paints.

A coat of clear varnish would add a nice finishing touch.

Tiny Tepees

Make a campsite of
these miniature shelters
and decorate them
American Indian style!

YOU WILL NEED

strong paper
compasses
a pencil
scissors
crayons
glue
wooden skewers

1   Set a pair of compasses 10 cm
    apart, draw a circle on stiff
paper and then cut it out. Reset the
compasses to 2 cm apart and draw
a small circle in the centre of
the large one.

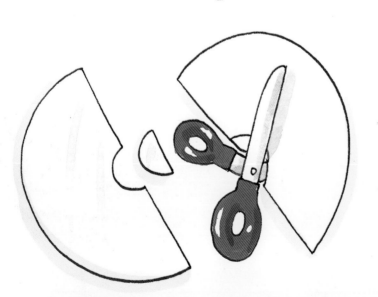

2   Cut the large circle in
    half; each piece makes
one tepee. Cut out the small
semi-circles and throw them
away.

14

3   Decorate one side of each large semi-circle with crayons or felt pens.

4   Curl a tepee into a cone and glue together the overlapping edges.

5   Cut three 11-cm pieces of wooden skewer. Glue these inside the tepee, so that the skewers stick out the small hole at the top.

You could cut a small slit and fold it back to make a door.

Space Rocket

This fiery spaceship will look great hanging in your bedroom.

YOU WILL NEED

a cardboard tube
kitchen foil
scissors
glue
crêpe paper
string or ribbon
compasses
thin card

1 Save a cardboard tube from a roll of toilet paper. Cover it with a sheet of kitchen foil and tuck in the ends neatly.

2 Cut narrow strips of red, yellow or orange crêpe paper. Gather the strips in a bunch at one end.

3 Tie a looped piece of string or narrow ribbon around the bunch. Thread the string through the tube.

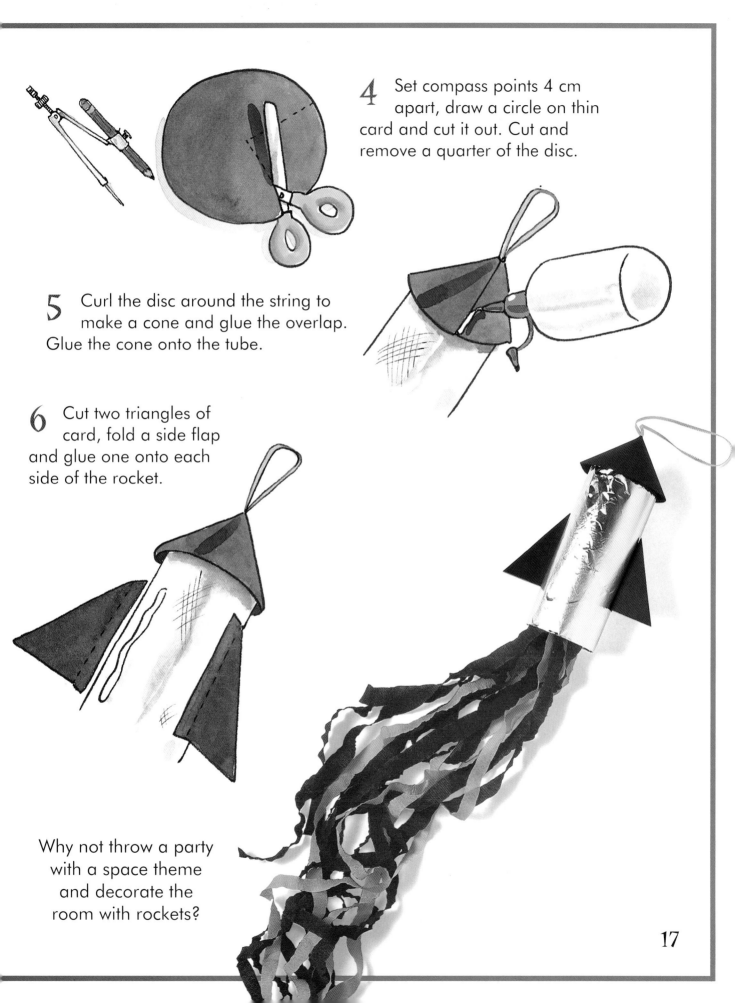

4 Set compass points 4 cm apart, draw a circle on thin card and cut it out. Cut and remove a quarter of the disc.

5 Curl the disc around the string to make a cone and glue the overlap. Glue the cone onto the tube.

6 Cut two triangles of card, fold a side flap and glue one onto each side of the rocket.

Why not throw a party with a space theme and decorate the room with rockets?

Bumbling Bees

You will need some odd bits and pieces to make these buzzers: all can be bought at craft shops.

1 Paint small polystyrene balls yellow. When dry, paint several black rings around each ball. Add eyes.

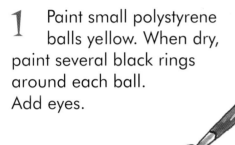

2 Cut pairs of wings from card. Make two cuts in the ball with a scissor blade and then push in the wings.

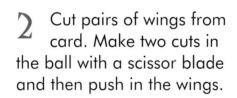

3 Unbend a paperclip and make a wire loop. Push the two ends into the top of the ball.

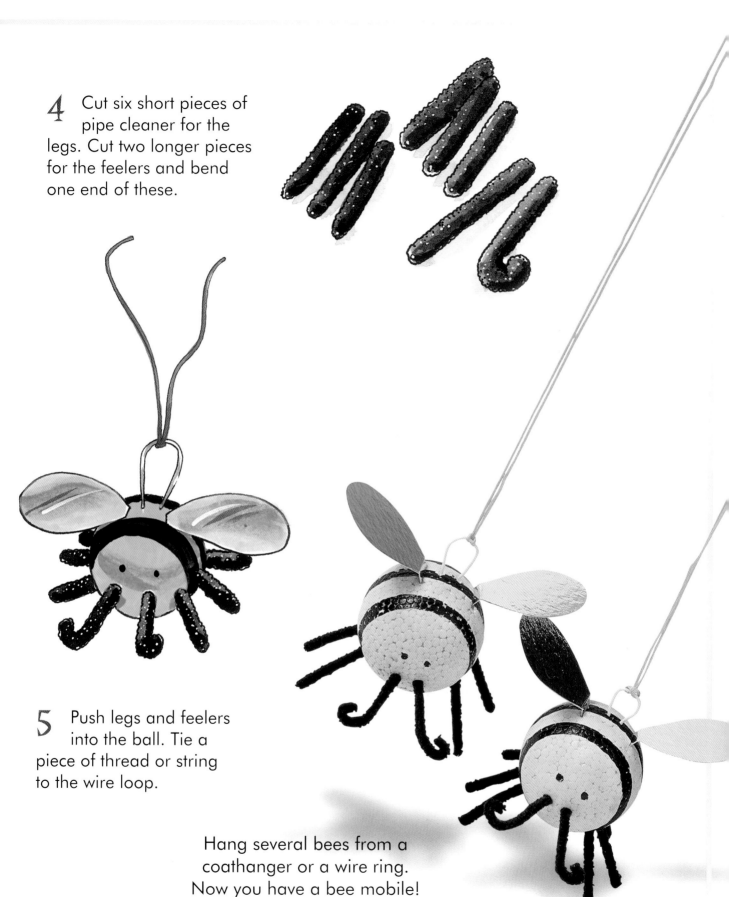

4 Cut six short pieces of
   pipe cleaner for the
legs. Cut two longer pieces
for the feelers and bend
one end of these.

5 Push legs and feelers
   into the ball. Tie a
piece of thread or string
to the wire loop.

Hang several bees from a
coathanger or a wire ring.
Now you have a bee mobile!

Make-a-Snake

This beautiful creature slithers when you hold him by the tail.

1 On a sheet of thin card, rule a series of lines 6 cm apart. Using a protractor, mark more lines at a 60 ° angle, 6 cm apart. You should now have lots of diamond shapes.

2 Cut along the lines and set two diamonds aside. Decorate the rest with a felt pen and punch a hole in either side as shown.

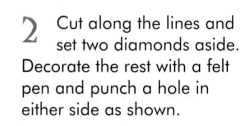

3 Bend each diamond into a ring and glue the overlapping ends together. These are the body segments or parts.

20

4 Pin the body segments together with paper fasteners to form a long chain.

5 Punch a single hole in each of the two remaining diamonds. Glue them into rings and pin one at each end of the snake.

6 On one end, draw two eyes and stick on a forked tongue.

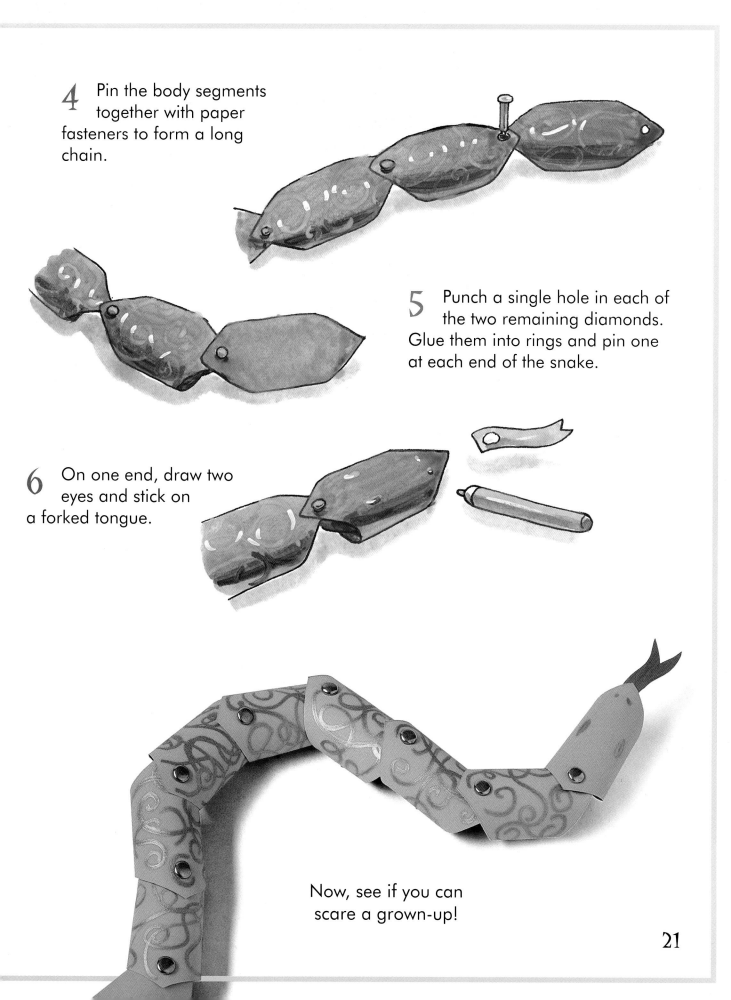

Now, see if you can scare a grown-up!

Monster Mask

With a little imagination,
a cereal box makes the
perfect disguise.

YOU WILL NEED

a cardboard box
scissors
a pencil
paints
a paintbrush
paper scraps
glue
a hole punch
string or elastic

1 Cut the back and base off a
box. Snip both sides at the
top, bend the flap and tape it so
that the box is now inside out.

2 Hold the box against your face
and decide where the nose and
eye holes should be. Mark these with
a pencil and then
cut them out.

3 Decorate the mask
with paint, feathers,
tissue paper, wool, sequins
or whatever you can find.

4   Cut a big nose or beak from coloured paper and glue it over the nose hole.

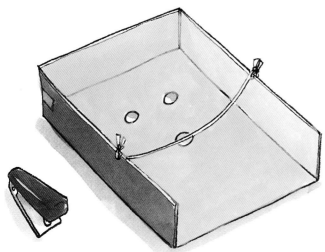

5   Punch a hole in each side flap. Cut some string or elastic to fit around your head and tie each end to the mask.

Now you're ready for a fancy dress party or just for a game of make believe.

Little Red Wagon

Collect enough matchboxes and you can make all kinds of trucks, cars and trains.

1 Paint the covers and trays of five empty matchboxes. Draw around a button or small coin on card and cut out enough circles to make wheels.

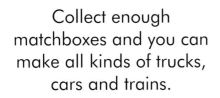

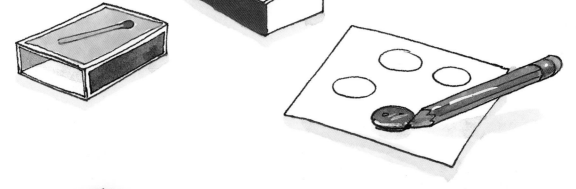

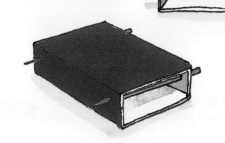

2 Use a skewer to make four holes in three of the matchbox covers. Poke a toothpick through each pair of holes.

24

3 Make a hole in each wheel. Push a wheel onto the point of each toothpick. Glue the ends if wheels are loose.

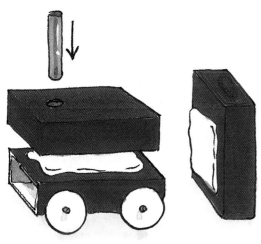

4 Glue two more boxes to a wheeled section as shown to make the engine. Make a hole in the top front and push in a piece of drinking straw for a chimney.

5 Smear the top of the other wheeled sections with glue. Lay a piece of string over them and stick a tray on top of each. Glue the string to the engine.

The more boxes, the longer the train!

Flying Saucer

This alien spaceship
not only looks good -
it also flies pretty well!

1   Glue two paper plates
    together so that they are
facing each other.

2   Cut the top third off a
    paper cup. Snip evenly
around the new rim and
bend the pieces back to
make lots of small tabs.

26

3 Put some glue on the inside of the tabs and stick the upturned cup onto the plate base.

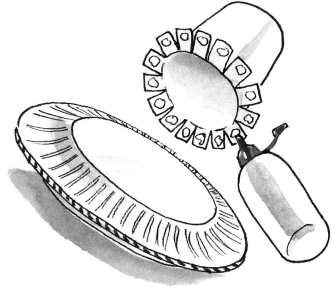

4 Colour the flying saucer with felt pens and stickers. Avoid using paint, as thin paper plates will go soft when they get damp.

Make sure to launch your spaceship outdoors rather than inside the house!

My Map

Can you make a map of the neighbourhood where you live?

YOU WILL NEED

a sheet of cardboard
paints
a paintbrush
boxes
corrugated card
glue
green paper
odds and ends

1 Paint a large sheet of cardboard green on one side and let it dry.

2 Paint a box to look like your house and glue on a folded corrugated card roof. Glue your house in the middle of the map.

3 On the cardboard, paint the streets around your house.

28

4 To make trees, snip along one edge of green paper as shown. Roll up the paper and tape it, then bend the snipped pieces into place. Glue trees onto your map.

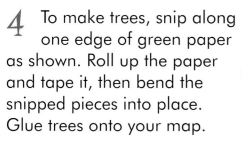

matchbox

sticky dots

pipe cleaner

cork

5 Add other buildings, such as a school, shops or your friends' houses. You could also add traffic lights or anything else that you see near your house.

You map should look different to this one!

Mobile Phone

Be the envy of your friends
with your own phone!

YOU WILL NEED
a long box
glue
tinfoil
a drinking straw
paper
a small button
scissors
felt pens

1 Find a suitable box. You can
shorten a toothpaste box by
trimming one end, cutting new flaps
and gluing them down.

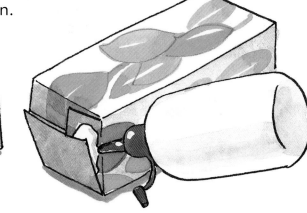

2 Cover the box with tinfoil.
Fold the ends neatly and
glue them down.

3 Punch a hole in one end
with the scissors point.
Push in a drinking straw as
the antenna.

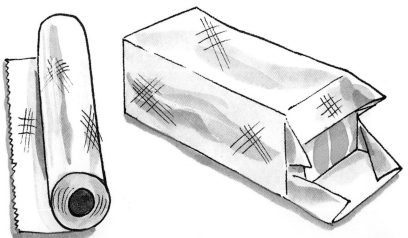

4 Draw a black box on some paper and colour it with felt pen. Cut out the box and glue it near the top of the phone.

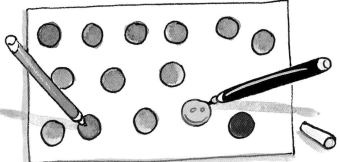

5 Place a small button on paper, draw around it and then colour it in. You will need at least 14 of these circles.

6 Draw a number or a symbol in each circle. Cut them all out and glue them onto the phone.

A hint: Using sticky labels makes this project even easier!

Sockaroos

This is a great way to use
those odd socks that you
find in the sock drawer!

1 Hold the sock so that the
heel is at the back of
your hand. Poke in the toe
to make a mouth.

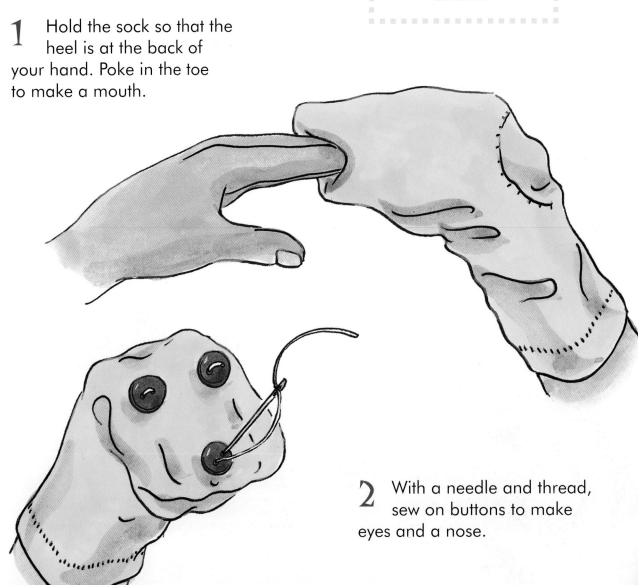

2 With a needle and thread,
sew on buttons to make
eyes and a nose.

3 To make hair, wind some wool around a piece of card. Tie a length of thread or wool around the loops.

4 Snip the bottom of the wool loops with your scissors. Sew the wig onto the sock using the two tying threads.

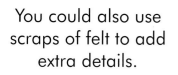

You could also use scraps of felt to add extra details.

Wind Wizard

This strange device will pick up the slightest breeze and whirl around madly.

1   Cut five cups from an egg carton and trim four of them so that they are quite shallow. Paint all the cups.

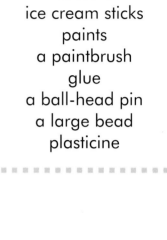

2   Paint two ice cream sticks. When they are dry, glue them to make a cross-bar.

3   Glue a shallow cup on each stick end as shown. Make sure they all face the same direction.

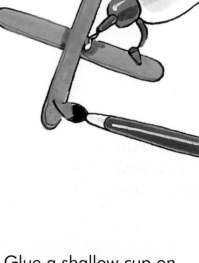

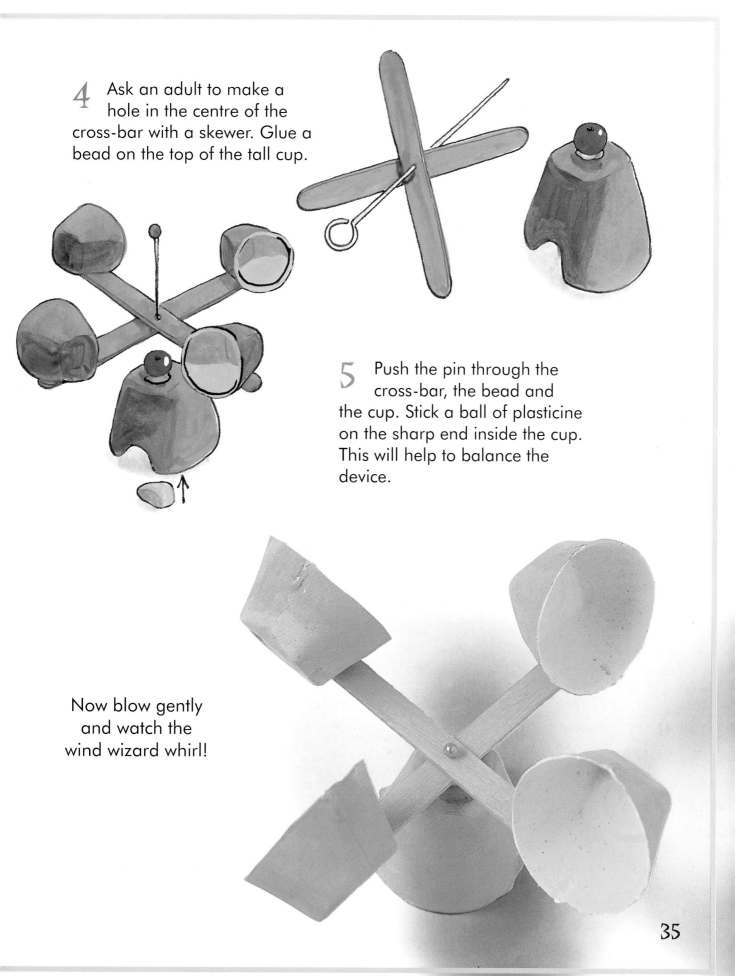

4 Ask an adult to make a
hole in the centre of the
cross-bar with a skewer. Glue a
bead on the top of the tall cup.

5 Push the pin through the
cross-bar, the bead and
the cup. Stick a ball of plasticine
on the sharp end inside the cup.
This will help to balance the
device.

Now blow gently
and watch the
wind wizard whirl!

Critter Candles

These cute candle holders are modelled with salt dough.

1 Mix ½ cup of plain flour with ¼ cup of salt in a bowl. Add ¼ cup water, a little at a time, until you have a soft dough. Knead this with your hands until the dough is smooth.

2 Set the oven to 120°C/250°F/ Gas mark ½. Roll a spoonful of dough into a ball to make the body and add a smaller ball for the head. Shape feet, hands and ears and press them in place.

3 Push the end of a candle into the dough and wriggle it around. Remove the candle and place the dough shape on an oven tray.

4 Bake dough shapes for three hours, then allow them to cool.

5 Paint the candle holder with acrylic paint and then with clear varnish.

Rabbit's ears were baked separately and glued on afterwards.

Pop-up Polly

Surprise your friends
with this kooky
puppet-in-a-pot.

YOU WILL NEED

a plastic bottle
a knife
crêpe paper
scissors
rubber bands
a wooden spoon
glue
thread
craft eyes or a pen

1 Cut off the top of a clean plastic
bottle by making a hole with
a craft knife and then using scissors.
You might ask a grown-up to help.

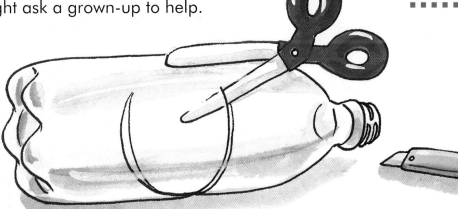

2 Wrap a piece of crêpe paper
around the bottle. Put a rubber
band around the neck and tuck the
loose paper into the bottle.

3 Cut a narrow section off
the crêpe roll. Tie a
thread tightly around the
paper loops and cut at the
opposite side to make a wig.

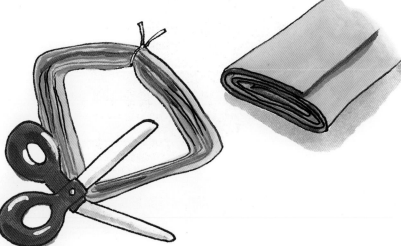

4   Glue the wig on the tip
of a wooden spoon.
Glue on some eyes or draw
them with a felt pen.

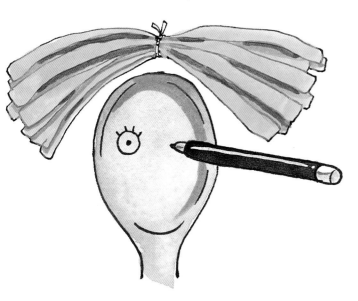

5   Slide the spoon into the bottle.
Cover the rubber band with a
crêpe paper bow.

A rubber band
here keeps Polly
in place!

Animal Ark

Collect boxes of
different sizes to make
this work of ark!

YOU WILL NEED

a shoe box
two smaller boxes
corrugated card
scissors
glue
paints
a paintbrush
a black felt pen
animal pictures

1 Snip the corners of a shoe
box lid and fold the sides so
that the lid is a bit smaller.

2 Place a small box, such as
a tissue box, inside the
shoe box and fit the lid section
over it to make a deck.

3 Paint the base of your
ark. Paint another
box, such as a pasta box,
in a different colour and
then glue it onto the deck.

4   Cut a square of corrugated
    card and bend it in half.
Glue this on top as the
ark's roof.

5   Draw port holes with a dark
    felt pen. Cut animal faces
from a magazine and glue them
on the ark, or glue on your own
animal drawings.

For the ocean, you could
cut up blue cellophane
or crumple a sheet of
blue tissue paper.

41

Weather Report

Look out the window
each morning and then
set the dial!

1 Set compasses to 11 cm apart
and draw a circle on card. Reset
the compasses to 4 cm apart and
draw a separate circle. Cut out both
circles.

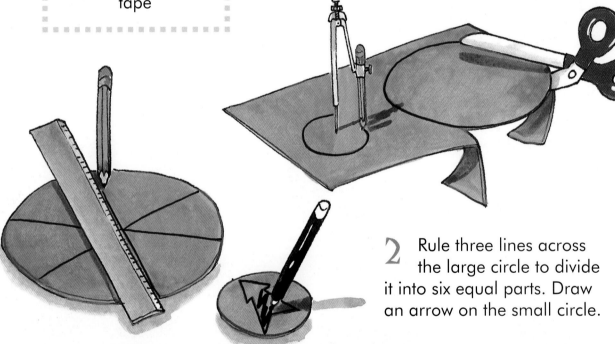

2 Rule three lines across
the large circle to divide
it into six equal parts. Draw
an arrow on the small circle.

3 Push a compass point through
the centre of each circle and
fix them together with a paper
fastener. The arrow wheel should
turn easily.

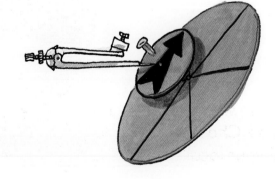

42

4 Tape a loop of thread or string onto the back for hanging the project. Plan your designs so the loop is at the top.

5 Cut up pieces of coloured card or paper and glue them onto each part to show different kinds of weather.

What's the weather like where you live? Choose pictures to suit your local weather.

Totem Pole

American Indians decorate huge wooden poles with carvings of animal and bird features. What will your totem pole be like?

1 Draw or paint an animal face on the back of a paper plate. You could glue on a beak or a snout made of folded paper.

2 Paint a long cardboard tube, such as a postal tube or wrapping paper tube. Draw some wings or arms on a long strip of cardboard.

3 Cut the lid off an egg carton. Cut and paint the bottom to make animal faces.

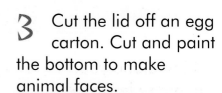

44

4   Paint or draw a pair of feet on the lid of the egg carton. Cut a hole in the top and push in the tube.

5   Tape the paper plate at the top of the pole. Attach the faces and wings and any extra bits and pieces.

Now stand your totem pole where everyone can see it.

Diorama Drama

A diorama is a model of a scene - under the sea, on the moon, or any place you like!

1   On one side of a shoebox, cut along both corners to make a flap.

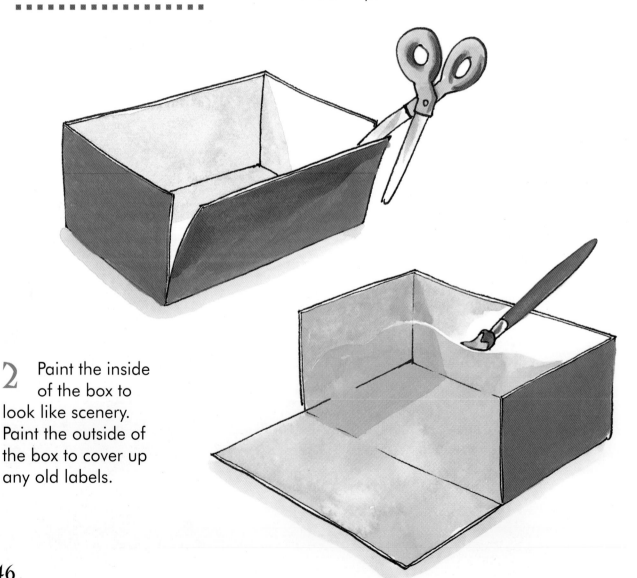

2   Paint the inside of the box to look like scenery. Paint the outside of the box to cover up any old labels.

46

3 Make trees and bushes with crumpled paper. You could use kitchen foil for a pond and some beads for flowers. Glue the bits and pieces in place.

4 Shape some figures with plasticine or modelling clay and place them in the diorama.

To store it away, simply fold up the flap and put on the box lid.

Index